# THE '101' SURVIVOR'S GUIDE TO THE CHURCH

# The '101' Survivor's Guide to the Church

A Handbook for the
Professional Religious
and the
Religious Professional

MARTIN WROE, NICK MCIVOR
& SIMON PARKE

MINSTREL
Eastbourne

*Text and front cover illustrations
by Simon Jenkins*

**British Library Cataloguing in Publication Data**

Wroe, Martin
    The '101' survivor's guide to the church.
    1. Humour in English 1945– texts.
    I. Title
    II. McIvor, Nick
    III. Parke, Simon
    828.91409

ISBN 1-85424-113-3

Printed in Great Britain for
Minstrel, an imprint of Monarch Publications Ltd
1 St Anne's Road, Eastbourne, E Sussex BN21 3UN by
Richard Clay Ltd, Bungay, Suffolk
Typeset by Nuprint Ltd, Harpenden, Herts

# CONTENTS

**1**

*A WORD OF EXPLANATION* 7

**2**

*THE CHURCH/ENGLISH...ENGLISH/CHURCH
DICTIONARY* 11

A comprehensive glossary of churchy language. All sorts of
ecclesiastical/religious/theological gobbledegook with crystal-
clear accompanying explanations. It will help you make your
own way through the foreign land that is church.

**3**

*A BEGINNER'S GUIDE TO PREACHING* 39

Ever had to preach but not had a clue where to start? Just
follow these simple hints—'obtained' by stealth from a
prominent Cleric Factory—and you can be strolling through
that special preaching experience.

**4**

*THE ASB: THE ALTERNATIVE SERMON BOOK* 47

Too tired to get a talk together this weekend? Stuck for that
moment of divine inspiration? Why not use one of our ready-
to-deliver, instant sermons for any occasion? Particularly
useful for those occasions which don't normally get a look-in
to church life—a General Election, for example.

**5**
## THE CRITICS: WHAT THEY SAID ABOUT CHURCH   65
What the critics said about church down the years and across
the bored. Do they like it? How should it be changed? What's
it all for anyway? Compelling reading for anyone in a
bookstore browsing through these pages and thinking of
buying this book. Go on—you can do it.


**6**
## THE BESTSELLERS   71
Stuck for that timely after-church word for your neighbour?
Confused and introverted by the service just over? Why not
engage in a stimulating conversation about the merits of a
Christian bestseller—even though you haven't read any? This
is just the section for you—pithy and occasionally tongue-in-
cheek resumés of the best and biggest in the world of
Christian literature.


**7**
## ECCLESIASTICAL SITUATIONS VACANT   79
Is God calling you? (If not why not?) If so, maybe it is to full-
time work for a Christian organisation, even a church? Ever
fancied a go at being Pope? Lots of jobs here—there's bound
to be one just for you.


**8**
## THE NOT TOO GOOD CHURCH GUIDE   87
An indispensable manual of every single church in the country
so that you need never be embarrassed about visiting a
strange one again. Easy-to-use guide tells you where to put
your hands, how many times they'll sing which chorus and if
the collection-taker will take no for an answer.


## GRAFFITI
*Not really a chapter at all. Just lots of comments by cool
dudes and smart dames down the years on life, the universe
and everything. Ideal for when you have failed to survive in
church—read these instead.*

# 1

# *A Word of Explanation*

Let's face it, church is not easy. It may have been around since BC
became AD, but just because church has survived us does not
make it any easier for us to survive church.

In fact most people don't survive. They prefer a lie-in or the
chance to wash the motor. Ninety per cent of British people never
go to church. Of the ten per cent of us who stick with it, well, we
often find church difficult: boring sermons, dreadful singing, cold
buildings, dodgy politics—and the awful coffee afterwards.

That's why we've come up with this **Guide to Surviving
Church**, a critical manual for those who don't want to abandon
the ship of faith, but could do with some light reading while the
storm rages.

Of course you may be a complete outsider to churchiness but
interested in what it's all about—which is why we've taken
nothing for granted. You'll need to know how church works, what
the rules are, what to do if, after your second visit, the secretary
asks you to give the sermon next week and how to get on if you
want to be a professional churchy—like an Archbishop of
Canterbury, for example.

We've also included a Situations Vacant section: perhaps at
some point you'll feel a call to full-time Christian service. Perhaps,

less loftily, you just fancy being a bishop because of the nice clothes.

We've dealt with the problem of funny church language: a complete phrase-by-phrase dictionary is included and we've specially commissioned from some of the country's leading churchmen a selection of sermons for significant cultural events or national occasions which are normally left out of the church calendar—a General Election, for example, or the Crufts Dog Show.

Preaching of course is a peculiar art with its own near-Masonic rules and rituals. But we are proud to publish for the first time extraordinary documents 'acquired'—ahem—from a theological training establishment (which the law will not allow us to name), giving remarkable insights into just how the art of preaching is passed on from generation to generation. Explosive reading, it reveals everything from how to get one of those funny sermon voices to how to command the interest of your congregation even when they haven't turned up again. Your unique A to Z for success as a preacher when the moment comes.

Of course surviving in church wouldn't be possible without some useful conversation ideas for after the service—it doesn't take long to exhaust all the variant weather conversations. That's why we've included a comprehensive list of Christian bestsellers down the years. Don't worry, you don't need to read them. Just memorise our short précis and that should enable you to bluff your way through most after-church conversations.

Inevitably any survivor in the church needs to know what different ecclesiastical traditions are likely to be present in a Sunday service. To that end we've included a remarkable selection of profiles of most of Britain's churches, the results of our pioneering survey which we publish in 'The Not Too Good Church Guide'.

Now you need never again break out in a trembling sweat as you visit a new church for the first time. No longer need you quake in your shoes wondering if you can bluff some tongues so that you don't look like a sinner if they bring on the glossolalia.

Fear no more the possibility of suffocation as the priest fires cannisters of incense-gas all around. Don't be scared to death that someone's word of knowledge about naughty thoughts must apply to you because no one else has owned up. With this handy reference guide you'll know how to act in advance.

Our hope is that this handy volume will prove an indispensable aid as you negotiate the trials and tribulations of Getting On in Church. But perhaps most important of all, a final tip: don't forget that Jesus never meant church to be as dull, predictable and institutionalised as it has turned out in most of the examples on offer.

When you're about to break down in desperation at your latest church experience, don't forget that you only have to go to one church once a week. Our Lord makes it his policy to turn up in all churches every week. Count yourself blessed.

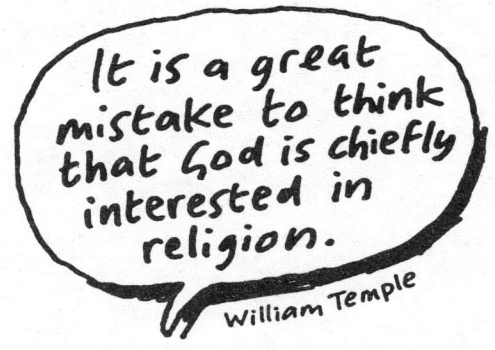

9

# 2
# The Church/English...
# English/Church
# Dictionary

Perhaps you've noticed that religious people, notably those in the Christian church, have a special language all their own. In fact it is as difficult to get on in church without a basic grasp of church-speak, as it is getting on in France without some simple French expressions such as, 'Où est the loo, please?' and that sort of thing.

The church can be a similarly foreign land to travellers not used to its unique terminology, its jargons and clichés. This short glossary should provide you with an indispensable reference tool as you struggle for survival in the church.

# A

AMEN
Hear hear; splendid; absolutely, old boy!; quite right too!; yes, yes, yes.

ALLELUIA
Term of praise and adoration—use it to express love for God. Works well sung. (See also H for Hallelujah.)

## ANGELS
God's motorcycle couriers; no request from the Almighty turned down; not human quite—not divine quite. Can get quite a few on a pinhead. Usually invisible, often turn up just when you need one—but you don't usually realise they were there until they aren't. (NB: some churches don't believe in them, others never think about them, some meet them for breakfast every Tuesday.)

## ANGLICAN
Beyond description.

## ARCH
Term of intimacy used by Anglican professionals of their earthly boss.

## AND FINALLY
Term used by preachers about halfway through their address.

## ANTHEMS
Lyrically brief, musically endless.

## ALL-AGE WORSHIP
Worship which no age likes very much.

## ARCHDEACON
The crook at the head of the bishop's staff.

# B

## BIBLE
The collected works of God. Believed to explain unusual story generally known as 'life'—in which black and white, man and woman, rich and poor all play starring roles in the strangest script, the longest film and the biggest budget production ever mounted. Unlike other interpretations of 'life', Bible version suggests that

when they roll the final credits up yonder the 'faith professionals' may end up with key-grip roles (what are they anyway?), while the faith-amateurs may get top billing.

**BLESSED**
Crucified.

**BOUNTIFUL**
What we call God when things are going well.

**BISHOPRIC**
Enough said.

**BREAD**
See OFFERING/COLLECTION.

## C

**CONVERT**
Person so embarrassingly excited at being a new Christian they try to make it compulsory for everyone else. Beware of them collaring

you in the bus-queue to tell you loudly about their night-life as a prayer warrior.

## COUNSELLING
When two gather for therapeutic pooling of ignorance.

## CHRISTIANISE
To make something essentially simple (like, 'God loves people despite their endeavours to be unlovable') into something quite complicated (like, 'Are you saved and washed in the cleansing rivers of blood, my brother?'). Alt meaning: to take out the interesting bits.

## CHRISTIANITY
Formerly simply called 'The Way'. Now sometimes more reminiscent of a bus stop.

## C. S. LEWIS
Mythical figure of spiritual and intellectual perfection reputed to have all answers to all questions. Supposedly based on Oxford don of the same name.

> **Mother Teresa**
> never reads a newspaper,
> never listens to a radio
> and never watches
> television... So she has
> a pretty good idea of
> what is going on in
> the world.
> _Malcolm Muggeridge_

## CONGREGATION
Group who gather each week to be reminded why more people don't go to church.
Alt meaning: the audience; the punters; the paying public; the pew-fillers; the home-crowd; the fans; the lads.

## CRUSADE
Tenth-century mission by the Genghis Khan School of Evangelism.

## CHOIR
Keenies, often musical (but not necessarily), usually in robes, found in choir-stalls.

## CHORUS
Song with good tune but no theology. (See also HYMN.)

## CHURCH COFFEE
Thin, faintly brown substance served after services. Tastes like nothing else. Not recommended.

## CROSS
Some pulpit, some throne.

## CHARISMATIC (non-religious)
George Best; Prince; Harrison Ford; Greta Garbo.

## CHARISMATIC (religious)
Opposite of anti-charismatic. May require an interpreter if in conversation—certainly if conversation is with God. Useful to warm up cold churches. Difficult when it all boils over.

## COLLECTION
Gathering of small change during church service for 'God's work'.

## CHAT
One-to-one, personal sermon.

## COFFEE
See CHAT.

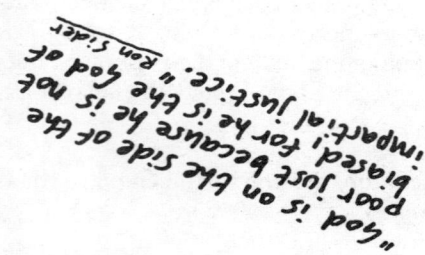

"God is on the side of the poor just because he is God of impartial justice." Ron Sider.

CONDEMNATION
Game played by many Christians, but particularly expertly by fundamentalists.

# D

DOOM
Feeling experienced by many church-goers in bed on Sunday morning. Usually followed by more sleep.

DEATH
A fact of life, but not the end of life in the Christian scheme of things. Generally believed to be final, but at least one exception suggests different rule. Simulated by many church congregations every Sunday.

DEACON
Like a 'gofer', but religious. Basically we...the deacon is...er...their function, well, that is—not to be a dogsbody, no, but rather to have a very real ministry. Yes, er.... (See also CONFUSED.)

DUTY
Job to be undertaken in public view with a look of martyred resignation.

DEMON
An angel gone off. Negatively-oriented spiritual power with friends in low places. May possess individuals who take them too seriously, but have a field day with those who don't take them seriously at all. Don't take to being laughed at or anything cross-like being waved in their vicinity.

*"Where there is no law, there is no justice."*
Big Bamboo

# E

EVANGELICAL
From Greek, meaning 'good news'. Should be a good news kind of person. In theory.

EVANGELISE
To explain the road to salvation in less than one minute without hesitation, deviation or repetition.

EROS
Widely assumed to be naughty-but-nice, but in fact can merely be extremely nice.

EYE FOR AN EYE
Old Testament approach to justice still adhered to by many Christians, despite later modification by Christ to the more difficult turn-the-other-cheek approach. Also very popular with Muslims.

EARLY FATHERS, THE
Technically, the late Early Fathers, as they are all dead. But still much earlier than us. Though not as early as St Paul, so perhaps the late *moderately* Early Fathers is more correct. Called 'Fathers', of course, because none of them were. Purveyors, like most of us, of deep insight and a load of tosh.

## EVERLASTING ARMS
Said to be 'underneath' and to belong to God. Ideal for human drop-outs of all kinds.
Alt meaning: favourite pub in the new Jerusalem.

## ELDERS
Christian pensioners who run non-conformist congregations. (See W for WARDEN for Anglican equivalent.)

## F

## FAITH (1)
All good Christians need this. Sort of like oxygen of the spiritual life—you gasp and give up without it. Contrary to popular teachings, Christianity is not just faith in a bunch of doctrines dreamed up by early church daddies, but faith in the closeness of Jesus, in the conviction that despite all the evidence to the contrary, at some point God will sit everyone down and say, 'Look, I can explain everything.' Faith that pleases this God does not have to be in a narrow set of statements to be ticked by the successful candidate. More like friendship.

## FAITH (2)
The outstretched hand.

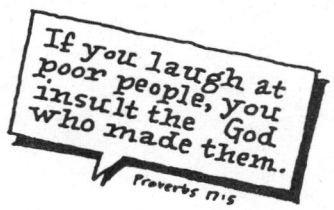

If you laugh at poor people, you insult the God who made them.

Proverbs 17:5

19

**FAT**
The outstretched stomach.

**FULLNESS OF TIME**
Never.

**FELLOWSHIP**
Group of people who enjoy talking about each other. Oddly enough used by Paul the apostle only in the context of suffering ('fellowship of sufferings').

**FUNDAMENTALIST**
Somebody who understands everything.

**FUN**
What fundamentalists fundamentally don't have.

**FOOL**
Anyone who follows Jesus Christ.

**BONKERS**
Anyone who decides against.
(Publisher: 'Er, F for Bonkers, boys?')

# G

**GIDEONS**
An association of Christian businessmen with terrible memories. They've left their Bibles in hotel rooms all over the place.

## GUITAR

Unique stringed instrument found in many churches and modified for use with three chords only. Believed by many to be created by God for youth services.

## GOD

God is a three-letter word. Without those three letters—or at least what they mean—there would be no book in your hand, no hand on your arm, no arm on your body, no body....

The Christian view is that God made everything up to start with and continues to make up everything as he goes along. In other words, if he had decided he'd had enough we wouldn't know it because we'd have been unmade up before we realised it.

The fact that our world is still here is testimony to God's penchant for what the Book (see B for BIBLE) calls 'longsuffering'. After all, just because God is a three-letter word does not mean that he is not also a four-letter word—LOVE.

Confusing, eh? But that's God all over for you. Miraculous.

## GUILT
A trusted retainer we keep on, because he's easier to handle than God's love.

## GABRIEL
An archangel. Also the sort of person most churches are seeking to appoint as their new minister or priest.

## GODPARENTS
Do you know anyone whom you can imagine still being on speaking terms with in, say, ten years' time? Choose them.

# H

*If people stop believing in God, they don't then believe in nothing, they believe in anything.*
*— G.K. CHESTERTON*

## HOLY
In communion with God.

## HUMBLE
In a right relationship with your neighbour.

## HUMAN
Someone who finds 'humble' and 'holy' rather difficult.

## HERESY
Disagreeing with John Stott (evangelicals) or His Holiness the Pope (Roman Catholics), John Calvin (the Free Presbyterians), the Ayatollah Khomeni (lots of Muslims), or Kenny Dalglish (Liverpool supporters).

## HERMENEUTICS
Like Herman and the Hermits, but not a sixties pop group.

## HETEROSEXUAL
What you need to be to keep out of trouble in most mainline denominations.
Alt meaning: someone pretending they're all right sexually.

## HIGH CHURCH
St Paul's Cathedral.
Alt meaning: those with a high view of the sacraments. Certainly over six feet, anyway.

## HI!
Expression of chumminess common to evangelical Anglican vicars as they meet you in the street.

## HYMN
Song with good theology but no tune (cf CHORUS).

## HER
Indoors—where many Christian hims believe that Christian hers should be kept.

## HOLY SPIRIT
God's kiss.

# I

## I
Common in extemporaneous prayers, as in: 'I really just want to say, Lord....'

## INFALLIBLE
Incapable of error.

## IAN PAISLEY
See INFALLIBLE.

ISN'T IT LOVELY?
Term used in spring/summer as church-goers enter/leave service to fill in silences. Thought to refer to weather.

INCARNATION
Difficult theological word to describe God's move from the lofty heights of the Godhead, heaven, Lord of the universe and all that...to the belly of a Jewish girl and life as a creature like the rest of us.

# J

JUST
See I.

JESUS
God's self-portrait.

True peace is not merely the absence of tension; It is the presence of justice.

Martin Luther King

JOYFUL NOISE
The sound of a musician who can't play.
Alt meaning: the sound of the church organ beginning the last verse of the last hymn on Sunday morning.

JUSTICE
What love wants.

*The kingdom of God is creation healed.*

HANS KÜNG

# K

## KOINONIA
Christian coffee-shop in Warrington.

## KINGDOM OF GOD
Where the poor are given riches, the mighty are humbled, the hungry are fed, the vain are disillusioned, the naked are clothed, the blind are given sight and there's dancing all night long to sixties soul music.

Christians live on its edge, in love with the idea but scared of the consequences.

The kingdom is here, but not all here—unlike Christians who are often here but not all there.

You can hear the kingdom on a good day. It's the sound of angels playing in a gospel combo, of saints marching in. The sight of all the colours bleeding into one.

# L

## LORD
Used regularly to punctuate extemporaneous prayers—in case God forgets it is he who is being addressed—as in, 'We do just ask, Lord, that, Lord, you will, Lord, bless, Lord, our Sunday School outing, Lord.'

## LAST TIMES
Periodic occasions in history when the world is about to end (until it doesn't), after which its proponents revise their theology and renew their pension scheme.

## LOVE
Rare substance. Believed to be what God is made of, and what he made people out of.

**LOVE MAKING**
What people make people out of.

**LIGHT**
What sermons generally obscure.

**LOST, THE**
People outside Sainsbury's on Saturday mornings being shouted at by men in sandwich boards and funny haircuts.

**LOVELY DAY, ISN'T IT?**
Term of after-church conversation to avoid talking about the sermon.

# M

**MOUNT UP WITH WINGS**
Climb on to a stage with Paul McCartney—theological implications unclear.
Alt meaning: to receive an unexpected cheque in the post.

## MAN OF GOD
Heavenly ranking bestowed while on earth. Just above 'man of prayer'.

## MAN AND GOD
Jesus.

## MINISTER
Non-conformist version of (Anglican) vicar or (Roman Catholic) priest.

## METHODIST
Unique approach to church-going pioneered by Robert de Niro-Wesley, known commonly as 'Methodist Acting'.

## MOVING INTO
Directional expression as in: 'Moving into a time of prayer/singing/having coffee/going to the loo/sleep . . .' etc.

## MIND
Something many church-goers have mistakenly believed they must hang up in the lobby on their way in to services. In fact Christianity is about wholeness which includes the development of everything up in your skull. A Christian mind ought not to sound a contradiction in terms.

## MALE
A slightly smaller version of what God is, according to most men in church.


## N

## NICENE CREED
The only fourth-century invention we're still using.

**NO**
Word believed by many non-Christians to define Christianity. And by many Christians.


# O


**OPEN OUR HEARTS**
Stop talking, will you?

**OFFERING**
You, in theory.

**ORGAN**
Large Victorian pipe instrument played by a fat lady at front of house.

**ORDINATION**
Two things happen at ordination: (1) Hands are laid on the candidate's head. (2) His backbone is removed.

The Moment of Ordination

Through violence you may murder the hater, but you do not murder hate.
Martin Luther King

## ORIGINAL SIN
It's extremely hard these days to commit sins with any degree of originality. But it doesn't stop us trying.

## OBADIAH
Not so much a *minor* prophet in the Old Testament, as a really *minimal* one. Bless him.

# P

## PCC
Group of geriatric Anglicans who agree to the incumbent's every whim.

## PEACE
The bit of the communion service when you try to appear interested in the person next to you.

## PARADE SERVICE
Theological nightmare. Dreamed up by vicar to attract locals.

## PRAYER
A list of ultimatums given to God when all other avenues have been exhausted.

## PRIESTS
See M for male.

PLASTIC CUPS
Created by God to ensure no one stays after the service. (See CHURCH COFFEE.)

PENTECOST
When God sets his friends on fire.

POPE
'His Holiness' to a billion Roman Catholics. 'The Beast' to Ian Paisley.

# Q

QUIET TIME
Ancient Christian ritual which involves making a cup of coffee, taking out a Bible, trying to find a comfy chair, wondering who to pray for, saying 'Amen' and going to the launderette.

QUESTIONS
What you get when you become a Christian.

*"Truth about society is best known at the bottom."*
Jim Wallis

# R

REALLY
Term of emphasis used by people who believe that God is in a hurry. Accordingly the pray-er cannot stop for breath or even to think of an interesting adjective when making representations before the throne of grace. Instead they insert the word 'really'

every couple of words: 'We really love you'; 'I really just ask that you will...'; 'Just really bless our time tonight.'

## RALLY (1)
As previous entry except posher. 'O Lord, we rally bless your name...'

## RALLY (2)
Event, often open air, organised by Christians to spread their good news to people who have yet to take note of it—or even any notice of it. Usually with loudspeaker—quietly spoken evangelists can use a microphone—and often in a big park. Common themes: Sin, Sin or Sin.

Lots of singing. If the rally is evangelistic then it often climaxes in altar call (see A for ALTAR CALL). If not evangelistic there is often no climax at all.

## ROYALLY
As in, 'life of'.

## RIPE UNTO HARVEST
Term of description for fertility—or otherwise—of soul of pagan contact. As in, 'Should get him saved soon'; 'She's on the brink.'

## REDEMPTION
God's idea.

## RELIGION
Man's idea.

## REFORMED
Often Scottish or German. Strict. Talk about John Calvin a lot.

## RECONCILIATION
'I'm in power and you'd better get reconciled to it!' (Alinsky)

**RAPTURED**
To be snatched bodily up to heaven.

**RUPTURED**
What happens if you get raptured in an awkward position.

**ROTA**
List of those due for rapture.

## S

**SACRIFICE**
Agreeing to be put on a rota.

**SOUND**
In agreement with me.

**SUZUKI YAMAHA KAWASAKI HONDA**

**SPEAKING IN TONGUES**
See previous entry.

**SATAN**
Also known as The Crowbar, because he separates people from people and people from God.

**SUNDAY SCHOOL**
A small therapy group comprising victims of parental church-going.

**STAINED-GLASS WINDOWS**
What you get after the Sunday School have painting lessons.

**SYNOD**
War zone.

## SACRAMENTS
Church history suggests that there are somewhere between nought and forty-three recognised sacraments of the church, indicating that they are either soul-bendingly important or completely peripheral. Or both. Or neither. Let the burning continue.

## SHARE
To whinge in public.

## SHALABALOM
Paul Daniels' magic word.

## SHALOM
God's magic word.

## SOCIETY
Place just outside the church which many church-goers, who go to meetings every day of the week, never actually get to see.

"Those who are comfortable, those who have possessions, and position, cry PEACE! . Those who are uncomfortable, those who have not, cry JUSTICE! ."

Andrew Kirk

## SELF
The bit many church-goers like to condemn all the time—evil, self-ish, generally not too good, etc. Also the bit Jesus said to love as much as our neighbour.

## SALVATION (1)
The benediction at the end of the service.

SALVATION (2)
The final hymn.

SYSTEMATIC THEOLOGY
'The devil's way to spread Christianity' (Munk).


# T

THUS SAITH THE LORD...
Don't you dare disagree with this!

TITHE
Conclusive proof that the average church-goer earns around £10
a week.

TIME OF TESTING
The minister's meeting with the scout master concerning the
National Anthem in the parade service.

TEMPTATION
The thought of where the scout master ought to go.

TRACT
Short but sensitively worded pamphlet that gently expounds a
person's need for God.

# U

UNDER THE BLOOD
The kind of easy-to-understand phrase tract-writers like to use.

USA
A country famous for its church-going and for the absence of God.

UNITY
Other people joining in with what we're doing.

# V

VERILY, VERILY, VERILY
All right, listen up...

VICAR
A qualified juggler.

VESTMENTS

Frocks for men.

VOLUNTEER
Somebody else.

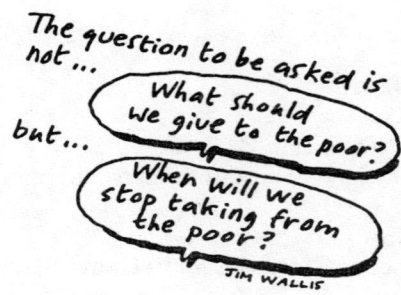

The question to be asked is not ...

but ...

What should we give to the poor?

When will we stop taking from the poor?

JIM WALLIS

# W

WHITHER GOEST THOU?
Minister who uses Authorised Version of the Bible, speaking to his son as he sees him driving off in the car.

WHITHERHELLDOYOUTHINKYOU'VEBEEN?
Same minister, as his son arrives back courtesy of a pick-up truck at 2 am.

WARDEN, CHURCH
Like traffic version but to stop you getting knocked down by mad drivers in church.

WALLET
Unique area in popular Christian theology: only place in entire universe and galaxies beyond where God is believed not to be.

WOMEN
Don't see under P for PRIESTS.

WOMEN OF PRAYER
Female version of men of God.

## WORLD
Good enough to be worth saving. Bad enough to need Christ to do it.

## WEATHER
Common topic of conversation after church by people too nervous or retiring to talk about something substantial, like what to do about the minister's sermon on Simple Lifestyles. For example, 'It's the greenhouse effect, you know...it's all in Revelation, of course.'

# X

## XSTATIC UTTERANCES
See S for **SUZUKI YAMAHA KAWASAKI HONDA.**

# Y

## YOUTH WORK
Talking to a young person in a down-to-earth, unpatronising sort of way.

## YOUTH RALLY
Talking to lots of people in a down-to-earth, unpatronising sort of way.

## YOUTH SERVICE
Patronising them again.

# Z

## ZION, LANGUAGE OF
See this entire section.

*"The God of the Bible is the God of liberation rather than oppression; a God of justice rather than injustice; a God of freedom and humanity rather than enslavement and subservience; a God of love, righteousness and community rather than hatred, self-interest and exploitation."*
ALLAN BOESAK

ZEAL
What young people ought to have.

ZEST
What they ought to wash with.

Once a man is united to God how could he not live for ever? Once a man is separated from God, what can he do but wither and die?
CS LEWIS

The primary form of love in social organisations is... Justice
WILLIAM TEMPLE

# 3
# A Beginner's Guide to Preaching

"WIDE-AWAKE" GLASSES
SLEEP IN PERFECT SAFETY
WHILE THE PREACHER GOES ON
PSALM 4:8

Imagination is more important than knowledge

ALBERT EINSTEIN

The historic art of preaching has a history almost as long as most of its sermons. As the great writer once remarked, 'Never in the history of boredom have so many been bored by so few for so long.' (This may not be a direct quote.)

Until the publication of this book it has never been clear just why so many preachers throughout Christendom sound so similar and so uninteresting for such similar lengths of time.

But the authors of this book have secured by stealth, in the higher interests of Truth, explosive lecture notes from a leading Preacher Factory which blow the lid off the whole ecclesiastical shebang.

Here for the first time we reveal the dark and shady tricks of the preaching game, offering remarkable insights into just how the art of preaching is passed on from generation to generation.

We hope that by reading these astonishing documents you will be able to succeed as a preacher when the moment comes.

## Preparation

One of the best times to prepare a sermon is in that limbo-land late at night, when, with your head on the pillow, you're drifting slowly out of reality and into unconsciousness.

However, if you do spend hours preparing, for goodness' sake make sure the congregation know you have. The congregation want to know that you know, so you must at least give the impression that you know. Or at the very least that you might know.

In other words, give them *everything!* Editing your extensive notes is a sign of weakness. We have a gospel to proclaim—*in full!*

**Delivery**

It's basically just a question of choosing a funny voice and staying with it. It's critical that your congregation recognise your preaching voice so that immediately you turn it on they know they are in the realm of 'the sermon' and don't attempt any dialogue with you, or even, Lord deliver us, answer back.

If they interrupt, not only is their mind in gear but—fatally— you will be completely thrown out of your stride.

The only criterion for the voice is that it doesn't resemble anything previously categorised as 'human'.

**Those crucial first few minutes**

A joke can be helpful early on, particularly if it is obviously at the expense of someone present. For example, 'I'm not saying this church is cleaned badly, but even the church mouse wears overalls these days.' Thus the church cleaner is humiliated and a dramatic tension is deftly created.

If preaching away, it is important to get the natives on your side. To this end, sexual innuendo can be helpful. For example, if you're a woman, you could dedicate the talk to 'the dream machine in the third row'.

If you want to get invited back to preach again next time the incumbent is absent, why not compliment his wife in the first row on her choice of bonnet—even if she does look like she's hosting an African safari on her head.

## Strategy

Because the punters love a challenge, don't let it be too apparent exactly what you're on about. Crucial to this strategy of course is that *you* don't know what you're on about. (Test: if you can sum up what you want to say in just one sentence, you're in grave danger of being coherent.)

## Content

Avoid stories at all costs. I know Jesus used them, but these days they could damage your image. To put it bluntly, in the West stories make people think you're a bit simple, thereby undermining your intellectual authority. To give the impression of brains and a sweeping understanding of the passage, you can either use the 'Three Points All Beginning with the Same Letter' model (which if Jesus had been a bit brighter he'd have done) or, just stuff the talk with references to the Greek, Hebrew, Latin and the Early Fathers.

Of course it's important to 'preach Christ crucified', etc. But let's be honest—it's also important to 'preach yourself'. Discreetly, of course. And with appropriate humility. (And let them *see* that humility.)

Religion is the fashionable substitute for belief.

OSCAR WILDE

## Dealing with disapproval

If someone is looking disapproving, worry not. Here is a four-fold fail-safe guide which you should never hasten to put into action.

1. Step authoritatively down from the pulpit.
2. Lay your hands firmly on their head.
3. Exorcise the demon of criticism from them firmly and audibly.
4. Return to the pulpit and continue.

There is unlikely to be any further incident during your sermon.

## Ending

Don't worry about how you're going to finish. It's really not important. The Lord will provide. (See RAPTURE, previous section.)

## To sum up

A classic sermon is comprised of five parts:

1. The fumbling. That uneasy opening section as you search around for what exactly—or rather inexactly—you want to say.

2. The beginning. We're ten minutes into the address now, a thought has just struck you, and you're away.

3. The middle. You say everything you know about the subject.

4. The losing of your way. Sensing unease, you opt for an unprepared tangent. Generally a mistake, but fun.

5. The gradual end, or disintegration. Involves the long haul back from the tangent, to the beginning thought. Most never make it.

❝ I hear and I forget.
I see and I remember.
I do and I understand. ❞
*CHINESE PROVERB*

## And finally

Don't forget this valuable homiletical gobbet. It's worth memorising and repeating to yourself under your breath as you start out on your sermon each week:

Tell them where you're coming from.
Tell them where you're going.
Go there.
Come back.
Tell them you've come back.
Tell them where you've been.
Tell them where to go.
Go.

# 4
# The ASB—
# The Alternative
# Sermon Book

## Note (for the preacher)

Too tired to get a talk together this weekend? Gardening been all too much? Kids been playing up again? Stuck for that moment of (divine) inspiration? Why not try one of our user-friendly, ready-to-deliver, instant sermons for any occasion?

After all, you've probably preached your way right through the Bible if you're worth your salt as a preacher, and all that stuff on the church calendar does get a bit dreary after 2,000 years.

Your job is to be relevant and up-to-the-minute with your Sunday morning homily—so why not try one of these pre-cooked tasties on your congregation. They're topical, contemporary and not too long. The idea is that you catch people's interest with a relevant event and then finish the talk before you lose them.

You should find something for most modern occasions.

## Note (for the churchgoer)

Can't be bothered to get along to church this w
you shouldn't miss out on the spiritual meat and
minister's sermon? Just select one of the following
the comfort of your own bed/armchair/foreign reso.
five minutes after your regular church service would i .y
begin. Guaranteed to do wonders for the old guilt pangs.

## Sermon on the occasion of an unusual personal experience

I wonder if, like me, you've ever stood up to your thighs in a river
amidst the uncertain rain of early spring, and watched the
conflicting ripples of the raindrops as they trickle from your chin
and hit the river surface? I wonder if you've ever done that?

Congregational Response: *[After some thought and in unison]*:
Not that we can remember.

Oh. Er…in which case, let's move on to our next hymn, which is
'Raindrops keep falling on my head'.

## Sermon on the occasion of having to pay the TV licence again

Last week I renewed my colour television licence. I took the old
crumpled one to the Post Office and exchanged it for a fresh,
clean one. And as I walked away from the Post Office that day I
thought, 'There's a lesson in that for all of us.' Are you feeling old
and crumpled this morning? If so, take heart, for you too can be
renewed.

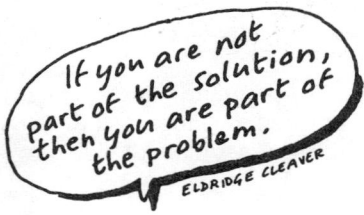

49

our faith is our heavenly television licence, then surely our songs of praise and worship are our spiritual TV licence stamps. So this morning *[remember: if it is an evening service, you could easily change 'morning' to 'evening' without the congregation knowing, and get double value out of this sermon]* I would encourage you to commit yourselves to those stamps, and to stick them firmly to the collecting card of salvation that is our hope of eternal life.

Or maybe your life seems drab and grey, and you are longing for a more real and more exciting Christian life. I am reminded of the time I replaced my black and white television licence with a colour television licence. The cost was higher, the commitment was greater; but oh, the wealth and variety of experience that became available to me.

Or perhaps you've sat here this morning and thought, 'Why do I need a heavenly television licence?' To you people I would say only this: a television licence may not look very significant, but how significant it becomes when the TV detector van comes to call, and when that inspector comes knocking at your door how glorious it is to say 'Yes! I have a television licence. I have the right to enjoy all the fruits of the British Broadcasting Corporation, and even ITV.'

Where will you be when the heavenly TV detector van arrives? Will you have your licence? Will you have the right to enjoy all the riches of the almighty broadcasting company? Or will you be consigned to the outer darkness of spiritual satellite broadcasting?

## Sermon on the occasion of a General Election

On Thursday last I cast my vote in the General Election. 'Who did you vote for, Vicar?' I hear you ask. I could of course remind you that it is an improper question, since we are privileged in this country to have a secret ballot.

But I shall on this occasion choose not to so remind you. Instead I shall tell you quite plainly that I placed my cross next to the candidate representing the 'Totally Loony Tipsy Truck-Drivers and Reduced Taxes for Well-Kept Lawns' party. 'Why?' I hear you ask. But I would like to turn the question back on you and riposte, 'Why not?'

You then reply, 'You're stark staring nuts, Vicar. You haven't got a full deck of cards. Your lift shaft is missing a couple of floors.' But then, my friend, aren't those exactly the words they used to describe our Lord?

Last Thursday you voted sensibly, responsibly, after prayer, reflection and serious thought. Last Thursday I voted like an idiot, like a fool, like a total turnip-brain of breathtaking proportions.

What were you? You were the good citizen. What was I? I was the Holy Fool. 'Come, follow me,' said Jesus. Last Thursday I understood the meaning of those words for the very first time....

## Sermon on the occasion of a General Election (Tory Party Version)

The General Election looms and soon we must all ask ourselves the question: where will I place my cross?

Will you vote for the confused mumblings of the centre, the godless heresies of the left, or the wholesome family values of the Conservative Party?

If we look at the kind of society God ordained for his people in Israel, we see that there is no National Health Service, no council housing, no unemployment benefit. Just a strong sense of family values and an 'eye for an eye' for anyone who didn't toe the line.

As Christians it is our duty to elect a government that stands for these timeless virtues.

In conclusion I will say only this: the kingdom of heaven is not a democracy. Only the Conservative Party has been built on this model.

## Sermon on the occasion of a General Election (Labour Party Version)

The General Election looms and soon we must all ask ourselves the question: where will I place my cross?

Will you vote for the confused mumblings of the centre, the godless heresies of the right, or the wholesome social concern of the Labour Party?

If we look at the kind of community Jesus' followers developed in the early days of Christianity, we see that there is a common purse, a policy of caring for the widows and the outcasts, and harsh consequences for those who put their trust in personal wealth. Witness the fate of Ananias and Sapphira. As Christians it is our duty to elect a government that stands for these timeless virtues.

In conclusion I will say only this: the kingdom of God is a community. Only the Labour Party is founded on such principles.

## Sermon on the occasion of a General Election (That Other Lot Version)

Well, there's an election coming up, and so much has been said already. The Conservatives tell you one thing and Labour tell you something else. But I always feel the truth must lie somewhere in between, although that's only my opinion.

Let's sing a hymn now, or does anyone have a better idea?

### Sermon on the occasion of a General Election (Monster Raving Loony Version)

Any of the above.

### Sermon on the occasion of a real old so-and-so dying

Today we gather to say goodbye to Reg. A man who many of us knew and, er, remember with much, ummm, vividness. A number of you have recounted to me at some length (and with some passion) a few of the more 'human' incidents in Reg's life, which leads me to believe that Reg will not be forgotten in a hurry.

He was after all a man. A man who lived a life, yes, but who has now in fact died. Once Reg was alive. Now Reg is not alive. Instead, he is dead. And we have gathered here to, er, record his passing—that I think we can say—and to pay our last, er, well, to say 'Goodbye', anyway. To say 'Goodbye' to a man who, by all accounts once was, but who frankly isn't now...er, so far as we can tell. Over to you, God....

### Sermon on the occasion of the vicar leaving

So. As the great and irreplaceable Moses told the desperately sad Israelites that he must leave them; and as the mighty apostle Paul, in that intolerably moving speech to the Ephesian leadership, bid goodbye to his weeping devotees; and as our risen Lord said farewell to his frightened disciples before ascending into heaven— so...I too stand before you for the last time, in this pulpit, before moving on to St Promotions-in-the-Suburbs, after many happy years here at St Struggling-in-the-Dumps. And I wonder how you will react?

Will you say, for instance, as the Israelites said, 'What will we do without you?'

Or will you say, perhaps, as the Ephesian elders said, 'Please don't go!'

Or will you simply cry out as the disciples cried out, 'Don't leave us, Lord, for we are lost without you?'

Will you perhaps be echoing one or more of these comments?

Congregation [*together*]: You must be joking, you silly old bore.

Er...precisely...that's the spirit!...yes, er...thank you so much.... Let us now sing, 'Through the night of doubt and sorrow'.

**Sermon on the occasion of being made Archbishop of Canterbury**

In the name of the Father, the Son and the Holy Ghost. Amen.

It's not every day you get made Archbishop, that's for sure. But just in case you ever get asked, I'd like to pass on to you this morning some words of advice, because, believe me, I've done it and I know what I'm on about. OK?

First, make sure there aren't any wars going on at the time. If there are, make sure you are struck down with a very prolonged attack of laryngitis, because it's really only when something big like a war happens that the Archbishop has to come down on one side or the other. Most of the time the country cannot remember what on earth an Archbishop is talking about—which is just as it should be. *[Professional smile.]*

Another way of making sure no one remembers what you are

talking about is to put what you are saying in such a complicated way that there isn't a living soul who can figure it out. It's not an easy task to come down really firmly on the fence about every issue and stay there—but it is the Archbishop's job, like it or not.

Secondly, don't forget to take your mitre off when you get into the limousine.

That's about it really. The rest is a doddle.

Now unto...er...there and back again, world without end. Amen.

## Sermon on the occasion of Trinity Sunday

It is Trinity Sunday and once again it is our joy and delight to celebrate the sheer 'Of-ness' of God. That he is, above all else, a God of 'Of-ness'. Pentecost reminds us of his ongoing 'Is-ness'; Good Friday, of his 'Was-ness' and his 'Has Been-ness' while Advent proclaims both his 'I'm standing Here in Front of Your Eyes-ness' and paradoxically, his 'Yet to be But not Quite Yet-ness'.

But for the 'Of-ness' of God, Trinity Sunday is surely the jewel in the crown, as each member of this divine trio gloriously demands to be Of the other two members, before they are From or With the other two members. In the divine economy of relationships, Of-ness precedes To-ness or With-ness.

And yet, my friends, isn't it true that in our lives it is very often the other way round?

*[The congregation shall at this point say, 'Errr....']*

Of what elevation to man is a method of broadcasting when you only have drivel to send out? What mark of civilisation is it to be able to produce a 128-page newspaper in one night when most of it is either banal or vicious and not two columns worth preserving?

Mahatma Gandhi

## Sermon on the occasion of a cabinet minister being revealed as an adulterer

The recent news that Mr _____ (insert relevant name) has been revealed as being the lover of a woman who was not in fact—or in fiction, for that matter—his lawful wedded wife, demands that we all ask ourselves a number of serious questions. The number is one, and the question is this: when we voted in this government as the Party of the Family did we know that in fact we were voting for the Party of Getting Your Mistress in the Family Way?

I think not, my friends.

It may be an old-fashioned word, but let's use it anyway— adultery.

This government has shown us the importance of the individual above anyone else, and shown us many other good and righteous things for which we must be truly grateful to them.

We have prospered under their governance. Certainly a slothful minority have complained of declining economic standards, of piffling details like slipping below the poverty-line etc, but if they won't get on their bikes and buy shares like everyone else it's not surprising, is it? I mean, really.

This government has shown us in short how to be a Christian country. But even God's instrument can be blunted as has been shown this week. Adultery is one thing, but getting caught is really going too far. However there is yet room for mercy, for forgiveness and for rehabilitation.

And there are precedents—King David for example. It didn't stop him being Israel's greatest leader. Which brings me to my main point.

We cannot afford to lose good people from our government just because they slipped up one night—or nights. They must apologise for the embarrassment caused to the government and get on with running this country as David did Israel.

Er. And not get caught again.

## 'Sermon' on the occasion of a stockmarket crash

MINISTER: Oh Lord, you did not promise us an easy life, and surely now our enemies afflict us sorely on all sides. Our share prices tumble, our creditors rave and our portable phones grant us no rest. Oh Lord, in this hour of our need, hear our prayer.
CONGREGATION: And answer it quickly.
MINISTER: When we are reduced to our final Mercedes
CONGREGATION: Sustain us, Lord.
MINISTER: When our loved ones are deprived of their designer footwear
CONGREGATION: Preserve us, Lord.
MINISTER: When our children have outgrown their swimming pools
CONGREGATION: Deliver us, Lord.
MINISTER: Grant unto us out of your manifold grace and abundance those cars...
CONGREGATION: Those large cars.
MINISTER: And houses...
CONGREGATION: Very large houses.
MINISTER: That declare your greatness to all that behold them, and make life jolly pleasant for us.
CONGREGATION: Amen.
MINISTER: Tonight's reading comes from the Gospel according to Mammon:

Blessed are the rich, for they inherited the earth some time ago, although the rest of you may buy shares in it so long as you can afford the broking charges.

Blessed are the powerful, but that goes without saying.

Blessed are those who hunger and thirst after money, for they shall be called enterprising.

Blessed are you when men envy you and admire you, for then you will have become a successful member of the competitive economy.

And as for the poor, the meek, the old, the sick, and the persecuted, you will get your reward in heaven.

This is the word of Mammon.

CONGREGATION: Praise the free market economy.

A city bullion broker decided to adorn his notepaper with a suitable motto and asked staff for suggestions. The best they came up with was...

## Ingot We Trust

*The Times Newspaper*

## Sermon on the occasion of Budget Day

Our gospel reading today is about the rich young ruler. Just one verse actually: 'Go, sell everything you have and give to the poor, and you will have treasure in heaven. Then come follow me.'

No further comment required.

Our final hymn before we pop off home and carefully ignore the reading is: 'Silver and gold have I none. But such as I have give I thee.'

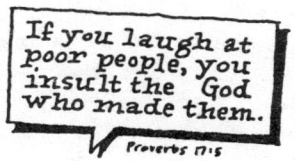

If you laugh at poor people, you insult the God who made them.

*Proverbs 17:5*

## Sermon on the occasion of the birth of test-tube babies

Today we hear news of the birth of test-tube babies, and I'm reminded of our own birth, first of water and then in the glorious second birth of the Spirit.

And you know, my friends, let's not mince words even though this is a delicate subject, in a sense we are all test-tube babies.

Don't look so shocked, my friends. *[Smile to reassure them.]* And in another sense we are none of us test-tube babies. *[Breathe as they relax again.]*

In the first instance none of us was conceived in a test-tube, but in the second instance all of us were. That test-tube was the person who told us of the gospel story, who showed us how to be saved, who alerted us to our mortality and lostness. Those people were our test-tubes by whose words our own second birth was conceived and nurtured until we were finally born again.

And so, my friends, there we have it. Not only are none of us test-tube babies, but in a very real sense we are all test-tube babies. And on top of that, if we are true evangelists ourselves, then we are also all test-tubes.

Thank you. And now I had better take a holiday. My retiring hymn is number 199.

## Sermon on the occasion of the Crufts Dog Show

I often think that church is a bit like Crufts. We have our different groupings, our different habits and different standards to attain, but all have the same supreme champion.

In a moment I'd like to look at that champion, but first I want to ask you a question: what breed of Christian are you?

Are you a rottweiler: big, powerful and perhaps a little intimidating? Or are you a terrier: small, noisy and irritating? Maybe you think of yourself as a labrador: faithful, gentle and kind. Or perhaps, if you are honest, you are something of a poodle: carefully groomed, beautifully presented but always a trifle ridiculous.

Today I want to tell you this: it does not matter. We are all doggies together in the great kennel club of heaven. Our breed is not important, it's the obedience trials that count.

Let's take a look at our champion. His parents were unique. His pedigree was unmatchable, yet never once did he claim the basket that was rightfully his. Instead he devoted himself to the obedience trial of life. And what was his reward? He was chained, muzzled and finally put to sleep. And today we feed on bread and wine as a sign that he is our pal. So now let us gather round this table and meditate on our supreme champion—a truly pedigree chum.

# FREDDIE STARR
# ATE MY HAMSTER

<u>Sun Headline</u>

**Sermon on the occasion of the Berlin wall being torn down**

As I watched those moving television pictures of the Berlin Wall being torn down by enthusiastic jerries recently, I was reminded of the wall of sin in our own hearts that needs to be torn down daily.

This is a rich and poignant illustration bursting with symbolism and spiritual allegories, but as I thought about it all in preparing my talk today it all seemed totally contrived and faintly ridiculous, so I'm afraid the sermon's a bit short today.

Er, that's it really. Sorry—do come again next week when I'll be expounding on another newsworthy event with significance for our everyday walk with the Lord.

**Sermon on the occasion of the latest famine reports from Ethiopia**

There will be no sermon today. Instead we will use the extra time for a longer collection.

MUST THE HUNGER BECOME ANGER AND THE ANGER BECOME FURY BEFORE ANYTHING WILL BE DONE? — John Steinbeck

## Sermon on the occasion of another baby being abandoned on the steps of the church

Today's lesson comes from the book of Genesis, chapter four. 'And Irad begat Mehujael, and Mehujael begat Methusael, and Methusael begat Lamech.' There was an awful lot of begatting in those days and it seems to me that there is a deal too much of it now. This fact was brought home to me earlier today when I arrived at the church to find an infant abandoned on the steps.

Naturally my first reaction was 'Why couldn't they have left it with the Methodists?' It was only when I looked for a second time that I began to realise the full horror of the situation. Not only would the verger have to brush the steps for a second time, but one of us would have to move the child, soil his clothing and consequently arrive late for the morning service. This callous disregard for our congregation demonstrates an attitude that is all too common among working people today.

Of course the church has a duty to the poor. Indeed, I spoke to one of them only last month. 'Tell me, my good man,' I said to him. 'Tell me how you think we, in the church, ought to teach you, in the lower orders.'

'Gawd bless you, guv,' he replied, 'but I wouldn't presume to give you advice.' And with that, he tugged at his forelock and went on his way. This fine fellow demonstrated how the working man can learn to behave if given the right example. But how do we, his betters, give him that example? First, we must remain rich, lest he forget that we are better. Second, we must discourage his improper traits with a sharp word and, where necessary, a sharp stick, and finally we must keep our begetting within respectable limits.

Now let us worship ourselves. Hymn 356.

Every 5 seconds a person dies of HUNGER

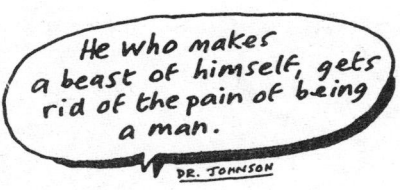

## Sermon on the occasion of a new government anti-drink/drive advertising campaign

I want us to think today of the occasion when our Lord miraculously turned the water into wine at Cana in Galilee.

It is interesting to note that the one miracle he did not attempt was to drive home afterwards.

A lesson for us all there, I feel sure.

Our final hymn is, 'Come on in and taste the New Wine (two glasses only)'.

God has no religion.

Ganghi

It may be the Devil
or it may be the Lord,
but you're gonna have to
serve somebody.

Bob Dylan

"We who advocate peace are becoming
an irrelevance when we speak peace.
The government speaks rubber bullets,
live bullets, tear gas, police dogs,
detention and death."

ARCHBISHOP DESMOND TUTU

# 5
# *The Critics: What They Said About Church*

'A visitor to a Cardiff church admired the altar flowers. Agreeing on their beauty, the verger added, "On Sunday nights they are always given to those who are sick after the sermon." '
*Daily Telegraph.*

'It seems to me easier to give sermons than to sit through them.'
Rabbi Lionel Blue.

'I have no objection to churches, so long as they do not interfere in God's work.'
Brooks Anderson, *Once Around the Sun.*

'The church which is married to the Spirit of its Age will be a widow in the next.'
Dean W. R. Inge.

'The church must be reminded that it is not the master or servant of the state, but rather the conscience of the state.'
Martin Luther King, *Strength To Love.*

'The church is, and will continue to be, persecuted as long as it does not accommodate itself to the whims of totalitarianism whether of the right or of the left.'
Arturo Rivera y Damas, Archbishop of San Salvador.

'A church is a place in which gentlemen who have never been to heaven brag about it to persons who will never get there.'
H. L. Mencken, *Prejudices*.

'We need to be the kind of church which tries to understand and obey the word of God for both rich and poor.... The church is one of the few bridges which can reach across to different sides of our polarised community. It is part of our reconciling task to help different groups to listen to what the others perceive to be happening.'
Bishop David Sheppard.

*South Africa...*
*...spends 4 times as much money on white education as on black.*

An inscription over a church door in Cheshire: 'This is the house of God. This is the gate of heaven. (This door is locked in the winter months.)'
*Daily Telegraph*.

'We do not want a religion that is right where we are right. What we want is a religion that is right where we are wrong.'
G. K. Chesterton.

'A great many more men would want to go to church if there was a law against it.'
Anon.

'People don't go to church, but they feel better because it's there.'
Jonathon Lynn and Anthony Jay, *Yes, Prime Minister*.

# 6
# *The Bestsellers*

Stuck for a word in season after church? Fed up with waiting around in embarrassed silence as everybody runs out of things to say again? You need a conversation about a Christian bestseller.

Don't worry if you've never read one (surely you've tried the Bible?). Use this easy reference guide to find out exactly what those bestselling titles by men and women of faith were all about. Memorise the briefs provided if you have to, but don't get into detailed conversation about any one title—you may be talking to someone who has actually read the book in question.

### The Old Testament *(Holy Script Publishing)*

Long but often moving account of one nation's journey to God...and then away again. And then back. And so on. Written in a distinctive 'biblical' style which has never been emulated (except by the next entry). The unusual mix of styles ranges from

horror stories to romantic literature; from erotica to poetry; from hymn-singing to Him-talking. Sales-wise a bit of a sleeper in the early centuries after publication—although strong Hebrew readership—but really took off after a crafty marketing ploy devised at a meeting of the Early Church Booksellers Convention, linking it up with the New Testament (see The Bible below).

## The New Testament *(Holy More Script Publishing)*

Sequel to the Old Testament, and continuing the story of how God's patience never seems to run out however far off the rails his friends go. Includes eye-witness accounts of central event in all history—the life of Christ. Opening with the Gospels, gripping, racy narratives by a selection of Jesus' close friends, the ordinary human ups and downs of an extraordinary divinity are revealed. The story they have called the Incarnation. Later chapters take up the successes and failures of the first followers of Jesus in . . . er . . . following Jesus. Material contains previously unpublished private letters of St Paul to early Christian believers—including his often frank and explicit descriptions of the things they got up to which they shouldn't have.

## The Bible *(Holy Double Edition Script Publishing)*

A gift set deluxe edition containing both of the above. The ultimate bestseller. Sales now approaching a billion billion copies and may soon surpass those of *Journey Into Life*.

Admittedly sales have been artificially inflated by the tendency of many Christian readers to have a whole collection of different versions. These may be different translations—like the New Parochial Universal French Window Cleaner's Edition (Red Letter)—or may be distinguished by the different animal skins used to cover them—like the recent Panda-and-Gorilla-Skin Edition of the Salvation Navy Christmas Day 1945 Commemorative End of the Second World War Children's Picture Bible.

Whatever the translation or the binding, one thing's for sure, it's the least-read bestseller of all time.

### The Complete Written Works of God

See above.

### The Cross and the Hot Water Bottle by David Waterson *(Thrillasinna Publishing)*

Unique story of one man's battle to bring peace and faith to the warring tribes of the Eskimo Indians whose survival in freezing conditions is entirely dependent on who has the hot water bottle.

Rev Waterson's success comes when he ingeniously invents an inflatable cross filled with...yes, you've guessed it, hot water. His missionary-fielders find this indispensable.

(Also available on film shot in high quality flared trousers.)

### Run Mummy Run by Micky Crud *(Thrillanothasinna Books)*

The unique story of one converted Eskimo's battle to bring hot water and a hot gospel to cold hearts and cold feet in dangerous, frightening, below-zero (etc).

### This Present Dampness *(Full Immersion Books)*

The epic tale of one small church battling against rising damp and a leaking roof.

### You, Me, Cliff, You and Me (and Jesus) *(Clifftop Books)*

Daily meditations on how to keep your skin wrinkle-free and your records at the top of the charts from one of Britain's best-loved confirmed bachelors. (Shadows, surely? Ed.)

### The Road More Travelled by Ivor Sequel

More map-work and royalties into your psychic problems.

### God's Hacker *(Smuggle Up Books)*

A true account of how Sister Andrew planted Bible verses on computers all over Eastern Europe.

### The Calmer Sutra by Rev Dr I. Amstuck and Mrs H. Elp *(Soul and Chips Books)*

A practical, understanding and helpful introduction to the sexual minefield by a former escapologist and his glamorous assistant. This edition not fully illustrated but always fully clothed.

### The Gift of Clean Clothes by Michael Othesbrush *(Vestment and DogCollar Publishing)*

Secular Diaries of Adrienne Plastered

The humorous, tongue-in-cheek tall tales and tittle-tattle of the girl you come to know as Adrienne, who is always... well, just a little tipsy. Amusing cast of characters. At the end of the book they all get saved.

### Knowing God Part 6 by J. I. Packemin

The Christian life made simple with complicated doctrinal explanations.

### 101 Things to do During a Dull Sermon by Martin Wroe and Adrian Reith *(Well Dodgy Titles)*

Extraordinarily moving book of how two young Christian men make money... er... discover their ministry.

### 101 Things to do With a Dull Church by Martin Wroe and Adrian Reith

More royalties, er ministries, as above.

### The Praise Principle by Dr Hal E. Lulajah *(Tongues Books)*

Have You Got A Hallelujah in Your Heart? No. Well get one under your arm at least, by reading this bestselling guide to praising and raving by one of East Grinstead's foremost exponents of the discipline.

### The View From the Cliff *(CliffTop Titles)*

The bestselling autobiography of a little-known tennis player.

## The End is Nigh by Sandy Wichboard

Open-air street witnessing. An indispensable manual for your instant embarrassment.

## Veal and the Art of Ministerial Maintenance by Professor V. Keen

Christian Cookery.

## The Riches of His Grace by Rev E. Nue

Zaccheus onwards—getting your heavenly rewards right here and now!

## Slim For Him by Ivor Thinwon

Ivor has shed more pounds for Jesus than anyone else. It was Ivor who coined the famous slogan of the Christian Slim for Him movement which cut a swathe through flabby congregations everywhere—'He must become greater and greater and I must become less and less.'

## Trust and Obey, There is no Other Way by Eileen Onim

Another weak pun.

## How and Where to Store Your Children's Toys Christianly by Pastor Ivor Textforanything

Paul's comment in Corinthians—'Now I am a man I put away childish things' (1 Cor 13)—is the keynote text of this brilliant theological exposition of where to put the kids' he-man and dumper trucks. Sensational reading.

**The Sheep From the Goats by Judge M. Ent**

Another pun.

**The Sleep of the Just by C. S. Ta**

And another.

**Finding Your Way Back Up the Road More Travelled by Earza Map**

One more.

**I Fell Over a Cliff and Lived by Eileen Dover**

Get it?

**Even More Surprised by Joy by Ida Shock**

And again.

**Holidays in the Holy Land by the Right Reverend Costa Packet**

One more.

**Judgement Day on High by Professor A. Judy Cashon**

That's it. (Honest.)

Still haven't found
what I'm looking for.
U2

# 7
# *Ecclesiastical Situations Vacant*

For many churchgoers the culmination of their churchgoing is when they become church-stayers. That is, they take a job within the church so that they never have to go again. Because they never leave it.

You may find one morning, looking at the vicar shaking hands with people after a service entirely led by members of the congregation, that the thought occurs to you, 'Why, I could do that! I've got a reasonable handshake. I could say, "And how are you, Mrs Blenkinsopp, this week? And what about little Beatrice's leprosy?" '

This thought may be significant. Many people have interpreted just such feelings as 'a calling'.

If you ever get such a calling you'll need a job in the church to be called to.

Here we select a few which you ought to think twice about.

## Have you heard the good news?

Are you willing to pass it on to others? Have you ever felt frustrated with your present job? Do you enjoy slogans like these? If so, we have the post for you. Contact the Missionary Tract Society, 99 Redemption Row, Easthampton.

## Evangelistic rock singer

We're looking for someone who can communicate with young people right where they were twenty years ago. Someone who can preach a three-point sermon after each song and still worry about making the message clear enough. Of course, a lot of people would just love the chance to climb onto a stage and strut their stuff in front of a dozen bored teenagers, but only a few can.

The successful applicant will have no musical ability and a wardrobe consisting exclusively of satin shirts, flared jeans and cowboy boots.

## Archbishop of Canterbury

Perks include extensive wardrobe including gowns, chains, frilly vestments, crosses and crooks.

Successful candidate will be able to do that funny sign with the two fingers of the right hand without trouble and without causing offence.

Accommodation available in pleasant palace in Lambeth area. Ideally situated for city and river walks and all ancient and modern conveniences. Also wide range of furnishings—notably personal seat in House of Lords for afternoon snoozing just minutes away.

(NB Women need not apply.)
*The Church of England is not an equal opportunities employer.*

## Hard working? Ambitious? Ordained?

We are a thrusting young fellowship who have enjoyed spectacular growth over the past four years. We are looking for a leader who can consolidate those gains and execute our 'strategy for the nineties' with a particular view towards Europe after 1992.

The successful candidate will have a proven track-record of selling pew-space and capturing business from competitor churches in the area.

## Imagine the following situation:

A church member comes to you and says she'd like to open a crèche for working mothers. She's put together a rota of willing volunteers to staff it, and there is an obvious need for such a service within the congregation. It will pay for itself, and the rooms she wants are not required for any other purpose.

Could you come up with half-a-dozen reasons why it's totally impractical? If so, you would be just the person we're looking for to be our next Church Warden.

## Huxter/conman/charlatan urgently needed

...to front nationally broadcast Christian talk-show. This position involves deft use of Christian language, extensive quoting of Bible verses, lashings of false humility, sincerity and crying to camera. The chosen candidate will have the ability to procure large sums of money from viewers.

## Salt of the Earth required

Plain ordinary Christian wanted. Extremely important position in God's plan to save the universe from itself. Job involves behaving like Jesus to the best of your ability so help you God. No salary. (*Rumoured to be reward in heaven, but we'll get back to you on that one.)

*Some want to live within the sound
Of church and chapel bell.
I want to run a rescue shop
Within a yard of hell.*
    ᴄᴛ ꜱᴛᴜᴅᴅ

## Could you be the next Billy Graham?

Tall, blue-eyed friend of President required. Experience with crowds essential—especially appeals over syrupy music. Would suit someone with background in sales or religion. Or both.

Basic salary of, well, we can't say, but it's modest. Commission considered.

Involves travel to funny places and looking interested when people say completely unintelligible things to you—prior experience as a Queen Mother would be ideal preparation.

The successful candidate will be working with a close-knit team who have designs on the world.

This is a scandal-free position.

## Happy pastor wanted

We are a varied congregation ranging from born-again fundamentalists through charismatic evangelicals to liberal gnostics. A lively debate between these different groups takes place every Sunday in the pews, corridors, toilets, pubs and streets surrounding the church.

Due to the unfortunate incarceration of our previous incumbent, there is now a vacancy for the post of pastor. The successful applicant will be free from doubts, difficulties or personal problems, happy, secure and immune from depression.

A background in the boxing ring or street-brawling would be an advantage.

*People don't care how much you know, until they know how much you care.*
*John Powell*

## Archbishop of Canterbury's special envoy

An important job involving travel, negotiations and a degree of personal danger. The successful candidate may well be accepting his last ever job in this life, as the position sometimes involves giving up your life in order to save that of others.

## Situation vacant—Calcutta

Do you like working with people...who smell horrible...and have nasty diseases? Is your idea of fun rescuing babies from dustbins?

No salary structure. Fat chance of promotion. Nothing but trouble ahead.

Extremely high job satisfaction—sometimes.

There's room for you on the streets of Calcutta and about ten thousand other major cities of the world.

No need to apply. Just take the job.

## Are you an advertising whizz?

Reached the top of the tree? Looking for a new challenge? The Church of England has got just the job for you.

We at the C of E, recognising that our goose is well and truly cooked, have decided to appoint someone to reposition the church in today's rapidly changing marketplace. The ideal candidate will have had success in selling fridges to eskimos.

## Could you suffer the little children?

Are you prone to guilt? If so, head for the Sunday School. No one else will. You will be working with unruly, disinterested, rude kids who, let's face it, are the church of tomorrow (and will probably be just as unruly, disinterested and rude then).

Perks: You get to miss the sermon.

*Love rejects the question —*

*What am I getting out of this?*

**The strict and very separate church of the isolated elect seeks to appoint a new minister. No one need apply.**

**The Church of England**

seeks to appoint for the first time a 'Financial Advisor to Hard-Up Clergy'.

Starting salary, in line with the rest of our bureaucratic appointments, will be £60,000 p.a.

As usual, the successful candidate should have a lot of experience and very little conscience.

Wife and 1000-pew church to support

# 8
# The Not Too Good
# Church Guide

There are nearly 60,000 churches in the UK, each with different ideas, emphases, styles of clothing and, er, buildings.

Surviving in any of them is not easy but we have conducted a unique survey of every single one as a way of providing you, the survivor, with a priceless reference guide.

Key:

minister has wet-fish handshake

minister has bone-cruncher handshake

minister hugs everyone

minister hugs and kisses everyone

minister's looking for a wife

organist can't play

man doing collection won't move on with less than a tenner

falling plaster

sub-zero temperature

 choir can't sing

 slide-off shiny pews

 worship

 membership

 healing

## St John the Power Evangelist (C of E), Wimberldon

Historical interest—no.
Services: healings, castings out, singing in tongues...you name it
we've got it.
Sermons: 2/3 hour minimum.
Dress: Top Man/C & A.
Hymns: no.
Choruses: yes, yes.

## St Simon the Simple

Building: super.
Membership: lots.
Worship: lots of that, too.
Remarks: we believe in preaching a simple gospel. For this reason
every morning service is based on John 3:16, and every evening
service on Revelation 3:20. The exception to this is Good Friday,
when we like to do sin. The vicar adds: 'Your coaches will wait.'

## St Redundant's, Relicsville

Historical interest: St Redundant's was built at a time in the nineteenth century when clearly everybody thought churches should be big, ugly and cold. We have tried hard to preserve that original intent.

Membership: (The vicar writes...) Er, it's just me, actually.

Worship: Well, I've sort of stopped having services because nobody really comes along. Hard to compete with the car-washing chores of a Sunday morning, eh? Anyway, if you ring in

advance I'll certainly open up for you and I'm sure we could knock a little church service of sorts together for you if you really wanted. I think I could remember how they go.
Hymnbooks: Ancient & Ancient.


## The Church of God's Bounty in the home counties

Building: big.
Membership: ££££££££.
Prayers: we prefer faxes.
Remarks: our teaching is based on the fact that God only grants wealth to those who deserve it. Of course it's true that his Son wasn't wealthy, but you know how it is with kids. For your free copy of 'The Tithe—God's Personal Pension Plan' write to the Rev Puller Fastbuck, Box 777, Maidenhead, enclosing £100 to cover postage and packing.

### The Harvest Time Church of the Restoration

At a cinema near you! Today.

### Holy Cowbatman, Gotham City

Minister: Right Rev Robin Boywonder, The Batcave.
Historical interest: founded in the late twentieth century, a pioneer of the thriving movement of 'theme' churches.
Theme: Batman and Robin.
Dress: leotards and coloured cardboard Batmobiles.
Hymns: just watch Batman videos.
Tune: 'De ne, na na, na na, na na...BATMAN!'
Church Motto: 'To the Batmobile, Robin...'
The Rev Boywonder adds: 'We are a relaxed congregation of Batfreaks and are experiencing genuine growth in numbers and commitment since adopting our radical thematic approach to replace the previous low-Methodist services. We have a completely unchurched congregation and are making genuine outreach gains into the local neighbourhood. As yet we have not raised the thorny issue of Christianity.'

### The Chapel of Salvation for Mankind

Principles: we are mindful of the fact that Jesus was a man who commissioned his men to preach the word to all mankind. This is reflected in our Sunday services when women are requested to keep their heads covered, their faces clean and their mouths closed. Other meetings are as follows:
Monday—Men's Fellowship
Tuesday—Men's Preaching Class
Wednesday—Men's Prayer Breakfast
Thursday—Men's Outreach Meeting

Friday—Men's Bible Study.
There is an additional counselling class each Saturday afternoon for men who find problems in relating to women.

## St Mary-may-not-have-been-a-virgin, Unshaw Street, Clericston

Historical interest: not much—more interested in making the faith acceptable today to the great unbelieving millions, and getting rid of dodgy 'supernatural' stuff that people find hard to stomach.
Membership: the whole wide world and everyone in it—it's just that they don't know yet.
Worship: absolutely, each to his or her own.
Sermon: 30 seconds.

## The Itinerant Church of the M25

Building: in keeping with the biblical practice of using other people's buildings, we are prepared to use any large warehouse or barn within reasonable distance of the M25.

Services (raves): 11.00 pm on a Saturday night. For further details ring 'Baz' the Church Secretary on his portable phone (no. 0860–144000).

Remarks: due to our somewhat unconventional meetings we encounter a certain amount of resistance among local residents. We regard this form of persecution as proof of our authenticity.

Motto: 'Let's party!'

## Stoleminster Cathedral

7.00 am—Matin Bells.
8.30 am—The Incensing of the Dean and Chapter.
11.00 am—Celebration of the Holy Wotsit and Things Like That.
12.00 pm—High Mass (Low attendance). Rite Boring.
1.00 pm—Reservation of the Blessed Parking Space (Just off Oxford St.)
2.00 pm—Confessions (Rite Interesting)
4.00 pm—Choral Evensong (Setting: 'The Awkward Choirmaster' in B#)
8.00 pm—Nonces.
9.00 pm—Complice.
10.00 pm—Complan.
11.00 pm—Complaints. (Setting: 'Why on Earth Do We Have So Many Flippin' Services?' by Stanford.)

## The Church of the Tongues of Zion

Worship:
Membership:
Healing Record:
Remarks: we are an ecumenical, Spirit-filled, charismatic, evangelical fellowship of born-again, pre-tribulationary

millennialists. We are committed to making the church relevant in our local community.